Think Differently
Live Differently
Study Guide

Bob Hamp

Printed in the U.S.A.

Table of Contents

> *I believe in Christianity as I believe that the sun has risen: not only because I see it, but because by it I see everything else. – C.S. Lewis*

The most important concept in this book is reflected in its title: Think Differently. Unfortunately, the concept is difficult to convey—not because it is complex, but because it addresses the *way* that we take in and process information. The *way* we think affects everything we consider. There is a profound difference between "thinking different" and "thinking *differently*." This study guide begins with *The Parable of the Code* because it clearly illustrates the distinction.

In the parable, every researcher is trying to uncover a new thought about The Code. In contrast, the seven-year-old boy doesn't approach The Code as something to learn, but something that invites interaction. As a result of the interaction, he is able to see everything differently.

The Parable of the Code is a depiction of the approach Jesus advocates when He tells us to repent—to think differently. He knows that the *way* we take in His teaching can either reduce His words to rules and laws, or it can help us digest those same words as life itself, the way He intended. Because *Think Differently, Live Differently* is designed to prompt life change, it should not be read as though it is just a book from which to obtain information. The goal is not to simply fill your mind with new ideas while you apply the same thinking processes that you have always relied upon. Instead, this book is intended to help you make a shift in the *way* you think.

According to 1 Corinthians 2:14, spiritual things are spiritually discerned. Spiritual truth is not processed by the brain, but perceived by the spirit. One sentence can have two completely different meanings and impacts depending upon the way the words are received. If you merely apply principles of learning while reading a book that is designed to transform your soul, you will miss its richest intent.

The focus of this study guide is not to assess how well you have learned the content of the book. Rather, it is designed to help you engage in conversations and relational interactions that reflect the truth it contains. The questions are intended to encourage you to explore your inner self and to process what you discover. Pay attention to the subtle and overt changes you experience in the way you see yourself, God, and most importantly, the connection between the two of you. Each chapter will help you shift the way you think about certain big ideas. Whether you do this study alone or with a group, check back to see how you think differently about the main ideas as you finish each chapter.

My prayer for each of you echoes Paul's prayer for the believers in Ephesus, written in Ephesians 1:17-19: May God open the eyes of your hearts and give you the Spirit of wisdom and revelation as you interact with the truth embedded in this book. May you see your true identity and inheritance, and experience the amazing, life-transforming power He offers to those who believe.

Enjoy the journey!

THE CODE

Like Atlantis and the Fountain of Youth, most people had dismissed The Code as a myth—another lost ancient treasure, hidden forever. From generation to generation, continent to continent, and culture to culture the whole human race seemed to know that a secret key to life existed, somewhere. They knew because they had heard about it firsthand, or their day-to-day experience confirmed their awareness that something like The Code must exist to make sense of it all. If such a document could be found and decoded, it would provide the key to virtually everything—peaceful co-existence, the restoration of everything broken, a better life on earth.

Though everyone knew that it must exist, no one knew exactly what it was. There were those who claimed to know, and their claim could not be proven wrong since The Code had never been found. No wonder that after centuries of conjecture about the legendary artifact, most people were doubtful when a team of experts claimed to have discovered it at last. They had followed clues from ancient documents that led them to a site in the Middle East. While excavating there they uncovered an artifact that was unlike any other, not just in its physical composition, but in every other way.

The Code was not written on a typical scroll used in antiquity; it was inscribed on a very strange material. Were it not so clearly ancient, it would have appeared that it was made of some sort of primitive plastic or acrylic. It was firm and didn't have the flexibility associated with paper, papyrus, or animal skin. It was solid, yet light could pass through it. The strangest aspect of this "document" was its shape—a slightly concave oval, just a little bigger than a football. This curvature made the writing on the document seem a bit distorted. Many of the scientists who examined it postulated that, at some point, the document must have been subjected to heat and had reached a melting point, causing the warped effect.

Evidence continued to indicate that this was indeed the document which had once seemed to be only a myth. Curiously, the writing spanned a number of centuries and was recorded in several languages. Therefore, the linguistic team had great difficulty translating the message, and the cultural interpretations were very complex. In response to these challenges, the greatest minds of the day were gathered to unlock the mystery of this "key to everything" code. Linguists, archaeologists, sociologists, anthropologists, geologists, and even some specialists in religious history all came together to solve the mystery of The Code.

The team's consensus was that the message written on this object gave helpful direction and instruction, but it did not seem to be the world-changing Key of Truth that everyone had been led to expect. It was meaningful and provided some insight, but many began to doubt whether this was actually the document the world had been hoping for. Either it was the wrong document or the expectations had been unrealistic. Surely no single code could change all that was wrong with the world! Nevertheless, the team kept working to decode the rest of the document.

One day, one of the sociologists was busy intently examining historical documents and cultural records. His son had accompanied him to work, and it wasn't long before the seven-year-old was drawn to the mysterious object lying on the table behind where his father was engrossed in research. The boy picked up The Code and, with great curiosity, began gently turning it over in his hands. What happened next changed everything: He placed it over his face like a mask.

Gazing through the object, the boy gasped, "Dad! Where did all these things come from?!" His eyes were wide with amazement and his jaw dropped as he slowly looked around the room through The Code. Then, he removed the object from his face and looked around a second time. "It's all gone!" he exclaimed, obviously puzzled. Again he lifted the "mask" to his face, in wonder. The room was once more filled with things he had not seen only a moment ago. The sterile laboratory was transformed into a garden-like setting with shimmering trees and plants—if you could call them that—growing everywhere. Familiar objects looked different when viewed through the lens of The Code, and the boy noticed a glow that shone around, and from within, his father. He marveled at several large shining beings, some of them nearly eight feet tall, standing by their side. As the boy took off the "lens," the appearance of the room returned to normal.

The child definitely had his father's attention now. The man approached the boy and carefully took the Code from him. Following his son's example, he placed the object over his face like a mask. At first, it was difficult to shift his focus away from the words and symbols he had been studying so intently, but when he stopped looking at them and began looking through them, he saw things in the room he had never seen before. Like the boy, he could see the towering beings and the plant-like objects. Then he noticed the light shining around his son, just as his son had seen around him. He had never witnessed anything like it! Even when he took the "mask" away from his face, his perspective remained changed. Having looked through The Code, he now knew the world around him contained much more than he could ever have imagined. He realized that the hidden key of the artifact was not only the ideas it contained, but also what could be seen when one looked through it. Interacting with the document in this way would allow people to discover a reality they had never before considered. The real power of The Code was not that it provided new information, but rather a new way of seeing.

The man excitedly shared the discovery with his colleagues. Strangely enough, not everyone who looked through this giant lens could see what the boy and his father had seen. In fact, when many members of the research team tried looking through the ancient material, their vision was totally unaffected. They were so trained to examine the language or the make-up of the thing itself that, even when they placed it over their faces, they could not look away from those elements. In other words, their way of viewing The Code didn't change—they were still looking at the words and symbols, instead of looking through the document. Eventually, some of the team realized their mistake and began to shift their focus from the micro-elements of the document and looked through The Code instead.

Sadly, those who could not see anything differently began to tell everyone who could see differently that they were delusional. The cynics believed the others were either deceived or deficient in some way. These men and women were never able to look past the object of their study to see the world that could only be seen through the lens, so they tried to lower the expectations of those who had not yet looked through the lens at all. They said that everyone was mistaken about The Code. As exciting as the discovery was, they insisted that it was not the key that would change the world after all. Yet, in spite of the cynics, those who looked through The Code in the same way the child had now had the power to see everything in a new way, to view the reality contained in a different dimension, and their world was never the same.

1. As you continue your journey to freedom using this study guide, why will it be important to remember that truth causes change in your life when you look through it, not when you look at it? Specifically, what will you keep in mind about the way truth causes life transformation?

_____

_____

_____

_____

_____

2. Do you tend to approach learning as simply the process of gaining needed information? If yes, take a moment to ask God to help you interact with truth over the next several weeks rather than simply study it

_____

_____

_____

_____

_____

Chapter One
The Parable of the Acrobat

He had to choose between the familiar reality his mind knew and the unknown truth that resonated in his heart.

GET IT GOING (for new groups)

What are you looking forward to most in this group?

TALK ABOUT IT

- What did you experience in your heart as you read this chapter?

- Which character in the Parable of the Acrobat do you identify with most? Why?

- Have you ever felt that "being yourself" wasn't an option, or that you needed to suppress your true self to please someone else? Why did you feel that way? How did you respond?

- The activities or experiences that make us feel most alive give us clues about our true identity and the purpose for which we were made. What activities or experiences make you feel most alive? For example, an engineer might feel "alive" when solving a difficult math problem, or a teacher might feel most alive when they see a student excel.

- The Parable of the Acrobat is a picture of the redemption that Jesus makes available to each of us. What concepts does this story convey about Jesus' message that are new or different, compared to what you've heard before?

- Read Matthew 25:14-30. In this story, Jesus describes three servants who were entrusted with different amounts of money to administer while their master was gone. How did each servant's image of their master affect the way they behaved and interacted with the master?

- Could your picture of God be inaccurate? How could thinking differently about God impact the way you interact with Him?

- What is motivating you to pursue greater spiritual freedom in Jesus?

Group Response – *Take a moment for each person to write down two things that they are hoping that God will do in their hearts over the next few weeks. Have one person pray and ask God to hear and respond to the individual requests.*

_____

_____

_____

_____

_____

_____

THINK ABOUT IT

What did you sense in your heart as you read this chapter? Do your best to put it into words.

_____

_____

_____

_____

_____

In the parable, the boy "became skilled at working the dirt" to earn the approval of the farmer. In what areas of your life do you feel that you are working hard at things that do not reflect who you really are, or seem to prevent you from pursuing that which is more connected with your life's purpose?

_____

_____

_____

_____

_____

The boy suffered a twisted ankle which later became a handicap to him. In what ways have you been wounded in your relationships, emotions, or self-image by a painful event? For example, _"My parents divorced when I was six, and the pain of it is still there,"_ or _"I was teased about my looks when I was younger, and it is difficult to believe that I am worthy of anyone's love or attention."_

_____

_____

_____

_____

_____

Has there ever been a moment in your life when everything you thought you knew about yourself or your life suddenly shifted, such as learning that you were adopted, discovering a family secret, or receiving a significant revelation from God? If so, describe the moment and the emotions you felt at the time.

_____

_____

_____

_____

What experiences, wounds, or "defining moments" do you think have shaped your view of yourself?

_____

_____

_____

_____

As you set out to learn and explore who you truly are, what are you most hoping for?

_____

_____

_____

_____

What are you most afraid of? Why?

_____

_____

_____

_____

_____

Ask the Lord for a picture of what He saw when He made you. Write down the thoughts or impressions that come to mind.

_____

_____

_____

_____

_____

_____

_____

KEY TAKEAWAYS

- Having a better life experience without discovering your true identity is not freedom.

- Until you discover your true identity through Jesus, you are separated from who you were meant to be and your true purpose in life.

- Living a life you weren't designed to live can wound you.

- Realizing that there is "more" in life means you will have to choose between settling for what is familiar and pursuing what is unfamiliar.

- You may be experiencing a tug-of-war between your head and your heart.

- Discovering your true heritage will reveal your true inheritance.

Chapter Two
Freedom and Bondage

Freedom is the ability to act and react in life as the man or woman you were created to be.

GET IT GOING (for new groups)

What was your favorite way to have fun as a kid?

TALK ABOUT IT

- What stood out to you most in this chapter? Why?

- Have you ever felt "stuck"? Describe what it feels like to be stuck.

- What do you naturally gravitate toward to get unstuck, *e.g.*, self-help books, conferences, talking it over with someone, etc.?

- Have your attempts to solve or improve a problem ever made the problem worse? How?

- There are three levels of bondage that must be negotiated in sequence in order to find true freedom: bondage to bad definitions, bondage to ourselves, and bondage to a variety of obstacles.

- "A bad definition of our target will always guide our best efforts in the wrong direction" (page 53). Has a bad definition of what it means to be free ever steered you in the wrong direction? In what way?

- You are in bondage to *you*. What do you think and feel when you consider this truth and the nature of the bondage it describes?

- Which of the three kinds of bondage do you tend to pay most attention to? Why do you think that is?

- What is the danger of giving the majority of our effort and attention to overcoming obstacles in our lives?

- Which of the three counterfeits described on pages 56 and 57 do you relate to most? Why?

- In what way does each counterfeit actually lead us away from God and/or true freedom?

- Before reading this chapter of *Think Differently, Live Differently*, how would you have described what it means to be free? Specifically, how has reading this chapter changed your way of thinking?

Group Response – *Ask God to help you set aside your definitions and methods for addressing obstacles, and invite Him to show you His truth.*

THINK ABOUT IT

What are the three most frustrating situations or obstacles in your life right now? List them below.

_____
_____
_____
_____
_____
_____

Briefly describe why each situation or obstacle is frustrating, and what you imagine that freedom would look or feel like in each situation.

_____
_____
_____
_____
_____
_____

Have you attempted to solve or improve these situations or obstacles in a way that has only made them worse? How? Can you see ways to solve them besides your typical response?

_____
_____
_____
_____
_____
_____

In what areas of your life have you defined freedom as an absence of boundaries, such as in your relationships, finances, or career?

_____

_____

_____

_____

_____

_____

How has reading this chapter changed your thinking?

_____

_____

_____

_____

_____

_____

Think of habits or repeated behavior patterns in your life that you find frustrating. Ask God to help you remember how each one first developed, and write down what comes to mind.

_____

_____

_____

_____

_____

_____

What real need or desire do you think you are trying to satisfy through this habit or pattern? For example, someone who is addicted to smoking cigarettes might discover that the real need they are trying to satisfy is not a need for nicotine but to find peace and comfort.

_____

_____

_____

_____

Ask God to show you how He sees each habit or pattern, and how He wants to meet that need in a different way. Write down what comes to mind.

_____

_____

_____

_____

Are you comfortable being alone, with only yourself? When you stop and *really* think about it, do you like being you? Why or why not?

_____

_____

_____

_____

Ask God to show you how He defines freedom, and what that means for you personally. Write down what comes to mind.

_____

_____

_____

_____

Consider this:

Jesus knew who He really was, and He allowed that awareness to guide the purpose and parameters of each of His relationships. When He comes to live in us, He helps us do the same.

> *Whoever confesses that Jesus is the Son of God, God abides in him, and he in God. And we have known and believed the love that God has for us. God is love, and he who abides in love abides in God, and God in him … as He is, so are we in this world.* (1 John 4:15-17, NKJV)

You have a new identity "in Him." The more you discover and embrace your new identity, the more you will experience the freedom Jesus came to give you.

> *Now the Lord is the Spirit; and where the Spirit of the Lord is, there is liberty* [freedom!]. *But we all, with unveiled face beholding as in a mirror the glory of the Lord, are being transformed into the same image from glory to glory, just as from the Lord, the Spirit.* (2 Corinthians 3:17-18, NAS)

Jesus said that He was anointed by the Spirit "to set at liberty those who are bruised" (Luke 4:18). A bruise is an internal wound; it can be seen by others, but can't be remedied from the outside. It must be healed from the inside out. Ask the Lord to show you any bruises you may have been carrying in your soul—your mind, will, and emotions—that have not healed. No one but God can heal your wounds because it's an "inside job." When you invite Him in and allow Him to work, His Spirit will move inside you and heal your wounds completely, as only He can.

KEY TAKEAWAYS

- The way you think about freedom will guide the way you pursue it.

- It is critical to have accurate definitions as you pursue freedom.

- You must negotiate the three levels of bondage in sequence to find true freedom.

- You may be stuck due to wrong definitions or wrong solutions.

- You must seek to think *differently*, not to think different thoughts.

Chapter Three
Who Are We?

If freedom is rooted in our ability to become ourselves, then we must know that our essential nature is spiritual and we are designed to remain in connection to the Source of life.

GET IT GOING (for new groups)

Are you related to any well-known historical figure, such as a king, political leader, inventor, or author? If so, who? If not, what well-known historical figure would you most *want* in your family tree and why?

TALK ABOUT IT

- Before reading this chapter, how would you have defined what it means to be "spiritual" or a "spiritual being"?

- How has reading this chapter changed the way you think about "spirituality"?

- Our identity is distinct from, but not wholly separate from, the Spirit of God. Describe why this means that freedom can only be obtained through spiritual means.

- Why can our thoughts, feelings, and actions deceive us into believing that we are someone other than who we are created to be?

- How can we be knowingly or unknowingly cooperating with this process?

- Read John 10:10 and 1 John 5:11-12. What do these verses tell us about Jesus' mission on earth?

- How does a new way of thinking about Jesus' mission on Earth change your understanding His purpose for you and His work in your life?

- John 6:63-64 (NIV) says, "The Spirit gives life; the flesh counts for nothing. The words I have spoken to you are spirit [breath] and they are life. Yet there are some of you who do not believe." According to this passage, why might some people not be fully experiencing the freedom that Jesus came to give them?

- What do you remember sensing or feeling when you personally connected with Jesus and invited Him to be your Lord?

- Why can't "aliveness" be obtained by *thinking different*—by adding new information or adopting a new approach?

Group Response – *Take a few minutes as a group to tell God how much you need His life within you, and invite Him to breathe into you today.*

_____

_____

_____

_____

_____

THINK ABOUT IT

Everyone has a *way of thinking* about who they really are. How has reading this chapter changed the way you think about your true identity?

_____

_____

_____

_____

_____

In what ways have you "cooperated with the process" of becoming someone else by defining your identity based on your thoughts, feelings, or behavior?

_____

_____

_____

_____

_____

What would you say are signs of "aliveness" in a person's life? In what area(s) of your life are you longing to feel "alive"? Why?

_____

_____

_____

_____

_____

_____

When you receive Jesus as our Savior, your spirit is brought to life by His Spirit. What does the following verse reveal about how His life invades your soul (mind, will, and emotions)?

> *In a humble (gentle, modest) spirit receive and welcome the Word which implanted and rooted [in your heart] contains the power to save your souls.* (James 1:21, AMP)

Both the Hebrew and Greek words that are commonly translated as "spirit" can also be translated as "breath" or "wind." In the Old Testament, the prophet Ezekiel faced a valley of dry, lifeless bones. What unfolded next was a foreshadowing of God's plan to breathe His life into those who are spiritually dead. This is how Ezekiel describes what the Lord instructed him to do:

> *"Prophesy to the breath; prophesy, son of man, and say to it, 'This is what the Sovereign Lord says: 'Come from the four winds, O breath, and breathe into these slain, that they may live.'"' So I prophesied as He commanded me, and breath entered them; they came to life and stood up on their feet—a vast army.* (Ezekiel 37:9-10, NASB)

Centuries later, Jesus, the Son of Man, said,

> *"I tell you the truth, a time is coming and has now come when the dead will hear the voice of the Son of God and those who hear will live. For as the Father has life in himself, so he has granted the Son to have life in himself."* (John 5:25-26, NIV)

> *"I have come that they may have life, and have it to the full."* (John 10:10, NIV)

Imagine the life of God filling every part of your soul (mind, will, and emotions). Now, write a prayer inviting Him to fill you with His life—His "aliveness."

_____

_____

_____

_____

_____

_____

_____

_____

_____

After writing, wait, then write down anything that comes to mind—what you believe He could be saying to you in response.

_____

_____

_____

_____

_____

_____

_____

_____

_____

_____

KEY TAKEAWAYS

- Who you are created to be is directly connected to your real Father.

- You have a Source and a self. Connection with the Source allows your "self" to become who you were created to be.

- You can become deceived about who you are by the way you think, feel, and act.

- Because you are made in His image, your true identity, which reflects His nature, can only emerge as He fills you with His life.

Chapter Four
What Happened? A Different Source

The knowledge of good and evil leaves incomplete people in charge of their own solutions. We think we see what's wrong and we think we see what would fix it. We think we know because we've connected to the knowledge of good and evil as our new source.

GET IT GOING (for new groups)

Which do you rely upon most for news and information—TV, radio, or the internet? Why?

TALK ABOUT IT

- As you read this chapter, what stood out to you most? Why?

- What are some ways a person might try to become self-reliant (their own source), such as by being a workaholic or a perfectionist?

- What ways have you tried?

- Before reading this chapter, how would you have defined "sin"? How would you define it now?

- Why is an accurate understanding of the problem of sin foundational to freedom in Christ?

- How has this chapter changed the way you think about what happened in the Garden of Eden?

- What is the problem that Jesus came to solve?

- "The human being is the only creature who can lie to itself and believe its own lie" (page 89). Like needing our glasses to find our glasses, our problem with the knowledge of good and evil blinds us to the real problem, which is the need to be freed from the knowledge of good and evil as our source. We are in bondage to ourselves and our own way of thinking. When has the problem of being in bondage to your own understanding been most apparent to you?

- Where can you find the solution to this problem?

- "Religious" behavior can be an attempt to fill the void in your heart (as opposed to a response flowing from the life of God within you). How can "doing the right thing" be a cleverly disguised method of self-reliance?

- "[Jesus] sets me free from who I have become and not just the habits of my past" (page 95). How does this truth change your understanding of what it means to be forgiven by Jesus?

- How does it compare with what you had previously understood?

- Many people have reconnected to God as their Source for their salvation but not for the transformation of their souls. Have you ever considered that God is not just the only true Source for your eternal salvation, but for your day-to-day growth and maturity as a believer?

- Why is it so common for a believer to remain separated from God as their Source related to life transformation?

Group Response – *Ask God to show each of you how the knowledge of good and evil has impacted your perspective, and invite Him to shift your source from yourself to Him.*

_____

_____

_____

_____

_____

THINK ABOUT IT

Have you connected with God as your Source of life by accepting Jesus as your Lord and Savior? If yes, describe your experience. If not, what is stopping you?

_____

_____

_____

_____

"[Jesus] sets me free from who I have become and not just from the habits of my past" (page 95). Reflect on this statement for a few minutes. Without mentioning your "bad behaviors," list the conditions of your heart from which Jesus has come to set you free.

_____

_____

_____

_____

What "bad" behavior(s) in your life have you thought of as "the problem"? What are these behaviors actually symptoms of?

_____

_____

_____

_____

_____

_____

_____

_____

Functioning under the blinding effects of the knowledge of good and evil, each of us become subconsciously convinced that we can fill our empty hearts by becoming, achieving, or attaining something else. We believe a lie that says we can fulfill our own need. These lies are what drive our behavior and who we ultimately become. In what ways have you tried to fill your own empty heart?

_____

_____

_____

_____

_____

_____

_____

_____

_____

What lies have you believed about yourself and/or what will bring you life? Ask God to show you what unspoken pursuits have been driving you, for example, to be respected, successful, rich/famous, or "godly." Write down the thoughts or impressions that come to mind.

_____
_____
_____
_____
_____
_____
_____
_____

Jesus has known all along that you are completely unable to be your own source and that you cannot make yourself "right" or become "good enough" to reconnect with your Father. He willingly came to freely exchange the death within you for the life within Him so you could have "life to the full." Have you ever felt ashamed before God or hesitant to approach Him because you thought you needed to "fix yourself up" first? What kind of thinking was this idea actually based upon?

_____
_____
_____
_____
_____
_____
_____
_____

How does understanding the real problem you've been wrestling with and the complete solution provided by Jesus change your perspective about His attitude towards you?

_____

_____

_____

_____

_____

_____

_____

Think about the full extent of Jesus' forgiveness. What thoughts or feelings arise in your heart in response to His gift?

_____

_____

_____

_____

_____

_____

_____

Jesus said that when the Spirit of Truth comes to live in a believer, He will guide them into all truth and reveal the Father's perspective to them. Ask the Holy Spirit to reveal the truth that God wants you to know that will make you free.

_____

_____

_____

_____

_____

_____

_____

KEY TAKEAWAYS

- The two main problems with humanity are that people are born disconnected from the Source of true life, and man has connected to himself as his own source.

- Your behavior is not the problem but the symptom of the problem—internal emptiness and death.

- Sin is not a wrong behavior but a condition of the heart.

- Jesus' forgiveness is not only for what you've *done* but for who you've *become*. When you receive Him as your Lord and Savior, He replaces the death within you with the life within Himself and reconnects you to the Father—the Source of all life.

Chapter Five
The Nature of the War

Often when we try to pursue freedom in our lives, we try to pursue it at the level of choice or action. When we do this, we significantly underestimate or even ignore the power of perception and desire. When we try to change our actions and choices without changing our perception, we set up a war within us that we are unlikely to win.

TALK ABOUT IT

• Have you ever thought of your journey to rediscover your identity and purpose as a war? In what ways has it actually *felt* like a war?

• Why is it important to understand that your struggle is not between good behavior and bad behavior but between truth and deception?

• What are some culturally accepted definitions and worldviews that keep us in bondage? For example, in many cultures living deeply in debt is acceptable, and premarital sex is considered "normal."

• How can our wills be used to keep us in bondage, even when we want to be free?

• In what areas have you tried to *will* yourself to act differently? What was the result?

• Why doesn't *willing* ourselves to act differently work in the long run?

- Describe a time when you observed that someone's behavior prompted a response from others that served to affirm their negative perception; for example, you watched a child who didn't think anyone wanted to play with them treat other kids rudely, so no one wanted to play with them.

- How did you feel when you saw this cycle at work in their lives?

- What advice would they likely receive about how to break the cycle?

- After reading this chapter, what do you see as the root of the problem?

- Do you see a similar circular pattern in your life? How?

- What would you say are common beliefs about God that are actually distorted perceptions about His nature?

- How would each of these distortions affect the way someone would relate to Him?

- "A common source of human conflict, or at least significant misunderstanding, is to interact on a topic that requires one way of knowing using the processes of an entirely different way of knowing" (page 112). For example, the way we know we are in love is a different *way of knowing* than understanding mathematical theory. Before reading this chapter, how would you have described what it meant to *know* God? How would you describe it now?

Group Response – *Together, or in groups of two or three, offer a simple prayer inviting God to change the way you know Him and His truth.*

THINK ABOUT IT

God promises, *"Call to me and I will answer you, and will tell you great and hidden things that you have not **known**"* (Jeremiah 33:3, ESV, emphasis added). The original language for the word *known* used here can also be translated *perceive, understand, discern,* or *to be aware of.* It is also used to describe intimate *knowing*, such as, "Adam *knew* Eve."

_____

_____

_____

_____

_____

_____

As you think about the following questions, ask God speak to you—for Him to deposit the concepts, ideas, and truths that you have not *known.* This is not an intellectual pursuit, but an invitation for God to supernaturally enable you to think differently than you ever have before.

_____

_____

_____

_____

_____

_____

At the root of our behavior are beliefs that drive our perceptions—what we perceive to be happening in a given situation. If what we believe is actually a "big lie," then what we perceive to be the solution will also be amiss. As you read this chapter, what "big lies" about God did you recognize in your own heart? *(A step-by-step guide is provided in Appendix A to help you identify underlying beliefs and perceptions that may be driving specific behaviors.)*

_____

_____

_____

_____

_____

What other "big lies" did you recognize about anyone or anything else, such as lies about men, women, spiritual leaders, success, relationships, etc.?

_____

_____

_____

_____

Ask God to show you the truth concerning each of these lies, and write down what comes to mind.

_____

_____

_____

_____

_____

What is a behavior that you'd like to change, but "can't"?

_____

_____

_____

_____

_____

_____

Why do you believe that you can't change, or haven't changed?

_____

_____

_____

_____

_____

_____

What other desire may be competing with or usurping this one?

_____

_____

_____

_____

_____

_____

Ask God to show you what core belief is at the root of the competing desire, and write down the thoughts or impressions that come to mind.

_____

_____

_____

_____

_____

Without filtering or "editing" your response, write down the first five words that come to mind that describe "the nature of God."

1. _____

2. _____

3. _____

4. _____

5. _____

Which words represent a "big lie" about God? How?

_____

_____

_____

_____

_____

_____

_____

What decisions or behaviors have been affected by your inaccurate perception? For example, if God is "angry," then I will work hard to avoid irritating Him by being perfect or by avoiding Him when I feel flawed.

_____
_____
_____
_____
_____
_____
_____
_____
_____

Without filtering or editing your response, write the first five words that come to mind that describe you.

1. _____

2. _____

3. _____

4. _____

5. _____

Ask God to tell you the first five words that *He* thinks describe you and, without filtering, write down what comes to mind.

1. _____

2. _____

3. _____

4. _____

5. _____

How do the two lists compare? Ask God to change your view of yourself—your beliefs and perceptions—to agree with His.

_____

_____

_____

_____

_____

_____

_____

_____

_____

KEY TAKEAWAYS

- You are engaged in a war to become yourself and return to God's original purpose for your life. The war is fought over *what* you know and *how* you know it.

- There is a progression that is ultimately based upon your identity and perceptions that drive your experiences and their impact. To break an unhealthy cycle, you must focus on the root beliefs and perceptions rather than the behaviors.

- The battle is not between good behavior and bad behavior, but truth versus deception in your heart and mind.

- There are different *ways* of knowing. Freedom does not come through an intellectual way of knowing but a spiritual one, through your connection with the Source of truth.

- By distorting your perceptions, the enemy can use your greatest strength (your will) against you and keep you enslaved.

Chapter Six
Life with the Acrobats

The more he got to know his true father, the more he learned about his true self.

TALK ABOUT IT

- In the parable of the acrobats, the young acrobat felt a range of emotions after his return to the troupe. What feelings did you most closely identify with in the story? Why?

- Have you ever felt that you didn't belong, or weren't good enough? When and why?

- "He applied himself diligently to learning these new skills in the same way he had applied himself to learn farming. Learn the task, pay attention to details, focus on the work—this had pleased the man who had raised him … he was going to get this right" (page 121.) What was the root problem of the acrobat's approach to acclimating to his new life?

- Have you ever applied the "old" methods of learning to your life in Christ? Specifically, how have you done that?

- What was the result?

- "The more [the acrobat] got to know his true father, the more he learned about himself" (page 122). In what ways have you associated the characteristics of your earthly father with your Heavenly Father, either positively or negatively?

- Read the following passages. What does each reveal about the nature of your Heavenly Father and the relationship you have with him?

  | Genesis 1:27 | Romans 8:37-39 | Ephesians 1:3-6 |
  | Ephesians 2:22 | Psalm 103:8-12 | 1 John 4:9-10 |

- Have you ever felt like you had discovered who you were only to find that you were not very good at it? How did it feel?

- How did you respond?

- Sometimes healing is painful, such as the pain endured while healing from a burn or undergoing physical therapy. The cure can feel worse than the wound! Have you ever had to endure pain to become physically well?

- What motivated you to continue the process when it was painful?

- How can this principle apply to the process of healing wounds in our souls?

- Have you been tempted to quit your journey toward freedom? What caused you to feel that way?

- Why have you chosen to continue the journey?

- What key moments or experiences have helped turn you back to the truth?

Group Response – *Take a moment to silently reflect, then have each person offer a one- or two-sentence prayer acknowledging something they love about the character of the Father, such as, "Lord, thank You that You are patient."*

_____
_____
_____
_____

THINK ABOUT IT

In what way does your journey to freedom feel most "unnatural" right now? Why do you think that is?

_____
_____
_____
_____
_____

What negative things have people said to you (or about you) that have discouraged you on your journey?

_____
_____
_____
_____
_____
_____

What accusations have you made against yourself?

_____

_____

_____

_____

_____

_____

Accusations can feel so true that we begin to agree with them. Read Romans 8:1-2 and 8:11. In your own words, write the truth presented in these verses. What is true about you?

_____

_____

_____

_____

_____

_____

What emotional pain, habit, or "character trait" in your life have you coped with for so long that you have become accustomed to it? If nothing comes to mind, ask yourself if there is anything in your life about which you say, "Well, you know me—I'm just _____ (clumsy/late/forgetful/a hothead/not good at school/quick to speak my mind)."

_____

_____

_____

_____

_____

_____

In what way has your pain, habit, or "trait" come to define who you are?

_____

_____

_____

_____

Can you imagine what it would be like to *not* be "that way"? Why or why not?

_____

_____

_____

_____

Read the conversation between the young acrobat and his father on page 125. As you read, place yourself in the role of the son and read the words of the father as though God is speaking directly to you. Then, write down what stood out to you as you imagined the interaction between you and God.

_____

_____

_____

_____

Read 1 John 4:13-19 in *The Message* version:
This is how we know we're living steadily and deeply in him, and he in us: He's given us life from his life, from his very own Spirit. Also, we've seen for ourselves and continue to state openly that the Father sent his Son as Savior of the world. Everyone who confesses that Jesus is God's Son participates continuously in an intimate relationship with God. We know it so well, we've embraced it heart and soul, this love that comes from God.

God is love. When we take up permanent residence in a life of love, we live in God and God lives in us. This way, love has the run of the house, becomes at home and mature in us, so that we're free of worry on Judgment Day—our standing in the world is identical with Christ's. There is no room in love for fear. Well-formed love banishes fear. Since fear is crippling, a fearful life—fear of death, fear of judgment—is one not yet fully formed in love. We, though, are going to love—love and be loved. First we were loved, now we love. He loved us first.

Ask the Holy Spirit to help you *know* the depth of God's love for you. What do you sense that He most wants you to *know* about His love today?

_____

_____

_____

_____

_____

The young acrobat reached a point where he was no longer motivated to become himself by an outside force—to impress his parents or peers, to prove a point, or to achieve something specific. He was motivated only by the power of the stirring within himself.

Ask the Holy Spirit to help you, and then take several minutes and *dream*. Suppose nothing else mattered to you besides following the stirring within. Who do you dream of becoming? Without "self-editing," write down what comes to mind.

_____

_____

_____

_____

_____

_____

KEY TAKEAWAYS

- Learning to live out your true identity is a process that begins with seeing yourself the way your heavenly Father sees you.

- You discover your true nature as you discover the true nature of your heavenly Father.

- Change, even for the better, can feel unnatural and painful at times.

- You may hear God through an unhealthy or inaccurate filter of your past, which distorts the message.

- Without realizing it, you may believe that your wounds or limitations are just part of who you are.

Shift the *way* you look at this page. That which is familiar will look completely new.

Chapter Seven
Shift

Truth is as much a way of knowing as it is what we know. Truth isn't the destination, but rather the compass that we travel with to get us there.

TALK ABOUT IT

- Describe an "Aha!" moment, spiritual or not, when you were suddenly able to understand something that you could not grasp, such as how to complete a complicated math problem or parallel park a car.

- What kept you from seeing or understanding in the first place?

- What shifted? How did you see old things in new ways?

- How did you feel when you finally "got it"?

- Read the paragraph on page 136 just below the subtitle, "How it Happened." What action words are included in the paragraph describing *how* the acrobat changed (*e.g.,* "stayed engaged")?

- What is the importance of each of the actions concerning change?

- What action words would you use to describe your journey so far?

- Three types of expectations that may cloud or block our view, like a tainted contact lens, are described in this chapter—familiarity, tradition, and rigidity. Which of these lenses can you relate to most? Why?

- What other types of expectations, or "lenses," can block our ability to see the truth?

- In what ways have you felt God lead you in your journey to freedom so far?

- How have you sensed Him with you—what does it feel like?

- Whose idea was it for you to become free to act and react as the person you were created to be?

- "Coming to know the truth … is surrendering to the viewpoint of One who is bigger, smarter, stronger, and kinder than we, and who will do for us the things we cannot do for ourselves in this battle" (page 137). To be healed from an ailing physical organ, we must surrender to the hands of a doctor or surgeon. What things, and in what ways, must we surrender to God to be restored, mentally, spiritually, or emotionally?

- What "lenses" might tempt us to resist or refuse to surrender to Him?

- "God is *with* us. He is here on earth. He is among the human race and He is ready and willing to act and to speak. He is present and He desires to interact with us" (page 143). Why is this truth foundational in our journey to freedom?

- Is it possible to become free while *not* believing that God is actively living and working in your life? Why or why not?

Group Response – *In prayer, express that you embrace God's way of thinking and surrender your own. Invite Him to reveal Himself to you.*

_____

_____

_____

_____

_____

THINK ABOUT IT

What traditions existed in your home when you were growing up?

_____

_____

_____

_____

_____

Would you say the overall effect of each tradition was positive or negative? For example, the tradition of eating together on Sunday afternoons may have been a positive tradition that encouraged unity as a family. However, "we don't talk about things like that" may have been a negative tradition that shut down certain kinds of communication.

_____

_____

_____

_____

_____

_____

What spoken or unspoken expectations existed in your childhood experiences? Consider what you were taught about how adults or children should behave, who should care for whom, what your responsibilities were as the oldest or youngest child, your performance in school or sports, etc.

_____

_____

_____

_____

_____

Ask the Lord to show you whether the expectations or traditions of your past have impacted your ability to see and be transformed by truth. Write down any impressions that come to mind.

_____

_____

_____

_____

_____

What does Jesus say about each of the "expectations" you listed?

_____

_____

_____

_____

_____

_____

"Truth isn't a destination, but rather the compass that we travel with to get us there" (page 136). What truths have become new "navigational tools" in the last few weeks? What are some new *ways of thinking* that have been birthed in your heart?

_____

_____

_____

_____

_____

_____

Revisit the parable of the acrobat in your mind. Have your hopes and dreams changed since the first time you read it? In what way?

_____

_____

_____

_____

_____

_____

Describe the feelings or desires that are awakening within you.

_____

_____

_____

_____

_____

_____

Read John 10:10. What is God's intention for your life? Ask Him to tell you what He thinks about your future and write down your impressions.

_____

_____

_____

_____

_____

An important part of being restored is surrendering to the Restorer. Have you resisted or found it difficult to surrender to Him? In what way?

_____

_____

_____

_____

_____

What do you sense is at the core of the struggle to surrender?

_____

_____

_____

_____

_____

Write a brief note to God expressing your desire to surrender to His truth and inviting Him to "open the eyes" of your heart to see as He does.

_____

_____

_____

_____

_____

_____

KEY TAKEAWAYS

- You can only act and react as the person you were created to be by being *restored*.

- Restoration comes through God's truth.

- Truth is not a destination; it is a compass.

- Your expectations are a mindset that may cloud or block your ability to take in the truth in a way that transforms your life.

Chapter Eight
The Bible: God Speaks

The Bible is related to truth in this way: the purpose, or end result, of reading the book should be an experience. Specifically, its purpose is to help us know and hear God more clearly so that we can experience Him and then share our experience of Him with others.

TALK ABOUT IT

- At the beginning of time, God launched a "multimedia campaign" to speak to us. Through what means have you heard God speak to you in the past?

- Before reading this chapter, had you ever thought of the Bible as alive—an interactive experience rather than an educational one? Why or why not?

- As depicted in the parable, *The Code,* the Bible can be viewed as something to be studied, such as a historical document, a textbook, a guide or poetry, rather than the "lens" of truth through which we become able to see everything else. How have you tended to view the Bible and its purpose?

- How do you see the Bible differently now?

- Specifically, how can we approach the Bible as something to be looked *through* rather than looked *at*?

- Refer to the illustration of the guitar amplifier on page 158: "We could debate this schematic diagram, study it, memorize it, or do whatever else we want with it. But unless we pick up an instrument, plug it in and play, we have completely missed the point of this complex schematic."

- In what ways do you "pick up an instrument, plug it in and play" concerning the Bible?

- Why do people have a tendency to become focused on the "schematic" (the Bible) and overlook or ignore its greater purpose (engaging with God)?

- Specifically, what filters identified earlier in this study can create this kind of obstacle?

- What do you usually expect to "get out of" reading the Bible?

- What do you think God wants you to "get out of" it?

- Why must we believe that God wants to *engage our hearts* to understand the true purpose of the Bible?

- Share an experience in which God's Word "jumped off the page," "resonated," or "spoke" to you. How did the experience change you?

- How has the Bible imparted God's *life* to your spirit in some way?

Group Response – *Have one person read the following passage, Hebrews 4:12 and 4:16 (AMP), aloud to the group as a declaration concerning God's Word and His grace:*

For the Word that God speaks is alive and full of power [making it active, operative, energizing, and effective]; it is sharper than any two-edged sword, penetrating to the dividing line of the breath of life (soul) and [the immortal] spirit, and of joints and marrow [of the deepest parts of our nature], exposing and sifting and analyzing and judging the very thoughts and purposes of the heart ... Let us then fearlessly and confidently and boldly draw near to the throne of grace (the throne of God's unmerited favor to us sinners), that we may receive mercy [for our failures] and find grace to help in good time for every need [appropriate help and well-timed help, coming just when we need it].

THINK ABOUT IT

What is the first word that tends to come to mind when you think about reading the Bible, such as boring, confusing, fun, or duty?

_____

_____

_____

_____

Ask the Holy Spirit to give you one word that describes *His* desire for you related to the Bible.

_____

_____

_____

_____

When you first sit down to read the Bible, how do you usually feel? What do you expect? For example, do you expect to be bored or not understand it, to learn something new, or for God to speak to you?

_____

_____

_____

_____

_____

_____

Why do you think that is? What experiences or beliefs may be shaping your expectation?

_____

_____

_____

_____

_____

_____

Think about the following question for a moment before answering: Do you *really* believe that you can hear God in a personal way through His Word? Why or why not?

_____

_____

_____

_____

_____

_____

"If you are looking, listening or tuned in to the many ways God speaks, I believe you will find He is deeply invested in communicating with you. If you are skeptical, analytical or looking for God to 'prove Himself', then you may find that you are deeply invested in communicating to yourself. Or if you are angry, hurt or disappointed with God, then your heart might be resistant to receiving *any* communication from Him. You might even have difficulty believing that He *desires* to communicate with you" (page 163). Which of these examples do you relate to, if any?

_____

_____

_____

_____

_____

Why do you think you feel skeptical, analytical, hurt, angry, or disappointed? What experience may have shaped your attitude?

_____

_____

_____

_____

What is the Holy Spirit saying to you about your feeling or experience?

_____

_____

_____

_____

_____

_____

"Jesus was saying to them, 'The Bible is part of My campaign to get you to meet Me, to talk with Me, to connect with Me. If you think knowing the Bible is the same thing as knowing Me, then you will think you have found real life, yet be fooled. The Bible tells you about Me, but the purpose of reading it is to engage with Me'" (page 157).

Write a brief response to Jesus' invitation to engage with Him through Scripture. What would you like to experience?

_____

_____

_____

_____

_____

_____

_____

What is He saying to you today?

_____

_____

_____

_____

_____

_____

_____

_____

_____

_____

KEY TAKEAWAYS

- The Bible is an important part of God's overall "multimedia" strategy to communicate with you.

- You can read the Bible through the wrong lens and totally miss its power and purpose.

- The Bible points to a reality that is greater than itself; it is meant to lead you to an experience with God.

- God's Word is alive; it has the capability to create whatever it speaks, such as "peace" or "planets."

Chapter Nine
The Gospel of the Kingdom

The Kingdom of God is a realm in which the atmosphere always reflects everything true about [God].

TALK ABOUT IT

- Before reading this chapter, how would you have answered the following questions:

- Why did Jesus come to earth? What was His message?

- What is the Kingdom of God? What is it like?

- In what ways do you now think differently about Jesus' purpose on earth, His message, and the Kingdom of God?

- What have you believed about the Kingdom of God that it is actually not true?

- God's original plan was for people to live in connection with Him, the Source, and to express His Kingdom on earth through that connection. How does understanding God's original intention and plan for restoration affirm that Jesus did not come to save us from bad behavior?

- Part of Jesus' mission was to reestablish our connection with God so His Kingdom can be expressed on earth. With this in mind, why is our behavior important?

- "[The Kingdom of God] is a Kingdom whose atmosphere is love because Pure Love rules, not just as an attitude but as a conquering force. The atmosphere is righteousness, not because a rigid set of doctrines are adhered to by the force of will but because righteousness flows out of accurate perceptions. The atmosphere is life, not just as the opposite of death but as the force of aliveness that conquers not only death, but sickness, depression and every other thing that would try to drain the life from God's sons and daughters" (page 182).

- Think of the aspects of God's Kingdom described above: Love as a conquering force, righteousness flowing out of accurate perceptions, and life as a force of *aliveness*. When you imagine living in such an atmosphere, what thoughts or feelings begin to stir within you?

- In "The Lord's Prayer," Jesus taught us to pray, "Your kingdom come, your will be done on earth as it is in heaven" (Matthew 6:10). How does the description of the Kingdom of God on page 182 affect your understanding of what Jesus encouraged us to pray for? What does God want mankind to experience on earth?

- Like a child who has difficulty understanding that life existed before they did, how does understanding the pre-existence and purpose of the Kingdom of God change our *way of seeing* our own lives?

- If we do not understand the pre-existence and purpose of the Kingdom of God, what will we miss seeing altogether?

- "The gift of God would *have* to be free, since mankind had no currency to exchange for it. All they had was themselves, and *they* were what needed restoring" (page 180). How does this truth destroy any belief that we could be or should be spiritually self-sufficient?

- How does this combat the commonly-held belief that God expects us to "get our act together" or become "good enough" for Him?

Group Response – *Using the Lord's Prayer as your model, pray and invite God to make His Kingdom seen through your life.*

_____

_____

_____

THINK ABOUT IT

Looking through the lens of the pre-existence and purpose of the Kingdom of God, think of all the reasons God wants you to be free to be who you were created to be. List as many as you can.

_____

_____

_____

Which of the reasons are most eye-opening for you?

_____

_____

_____

Which bring a greater sense of purpose or motivation to your life?

_____

_____

_____

_____

In your own words, describe why Jesus wants you to be free from self-destructive behaviors (even those that you do not perceive to be self-destructive).

_____

_____

_____

_____

_____

Read the story of the woman caught in adultery in John 8:1-11 (or refer to the story on page 181). Imagine yourself as the woman caught in sin. What have you done that has caused you to hear voices of accusation, either real or imagined?

_____

_____

_____

_____

_____

In the past, how have you imagined that Jesus responds to you and your sinfulness, especially related to the area you listed above? (Has He been angry? Impatient? Forgiving?)

_____

_____

_____

_____

_____

_____

Read the story again, replacing the woman with yourself and her sin with your bad thing. According to the story, how does Jesus respond to you? To your sin? Listen to His voice in your heart. What is He saying to you?

_____

_____

_____

_____

_____

_____

In writing, respond to what He is saying to you.

_____

_____

_____

_____

_____

Read Ephesians 1:17-19. How has God "enlightened the eyes of your heart" through this chapter?

_____

_____

_____

_____

_____

_____

How do you see yourself differently in light of His Kingdom?

_____

_____

_____

_____

_____

_____

_____

_____

Ask the Holy Spirit to show you what personal message Jesus wants to give you today. Write down what comes to mind. Do not "edit" your thoughts.

_____

_____

_____

_____

_____

_____

_____

_____

_____

_____

_____

_____

_____

KEY TAKEAWAYS

- Jesus didn't come to tell you the proper way to behave, but to do for you what was impossible for you to do for yourself.

- You must look at the God's pre-existing story of His Kingdom to have a greater understanding of His purposes for your life.

- The Kingdom of God reflects the nature of God in every way.

- God intended to express His Kingdom on earth through His connection with people. That connection was lost in the Garden of Eden, and is what Jesus came to restore.

- The Kingdom of God is all around you but without the right "receiver," which is restored by Jesus through your faith in Him, you can't "tune in" to its frequency.

- Your role is to enter God's Kingdom by faith and allow its atmosphere to change and restore you.

Chapter Ten
Freedom from Obstacles

We overcome evil with good—not our own idea of goodness, which contains no power, but instead with God's goodness powerfully operating through us.

TALK ABOUT IT

- As you read this chapter, what stood out to you most? Why?

- On page 195 there is a description of questions or feelings that indicate a state of internal disagreement. In what areas of your life have you sensed a state of internal disagreement?

- Why do you think that is?

- How does the sense of internal disagreement make you feel?

- When you were growing up, what were you taught concerning how to manage your feelings?

- How do you tend to deal with your feelings now? For example, do you dismiss or deny your feelings, are you *led* by your feelings, or do you always believe they are the truth?

- As you read the chapter, which of the common obstacles did you identify with most: core lies, soul wounds, life patterns, or spiritual obstacles? Why?

- Life patterns are often easy to spot in other people's lives and difficult to identify in our own. What common life patterns have you observed in others?

- What kind of advice do people dealing with life patterns most often receive?

- What is the truth about the root of life patterns?

- Why are spiritual forces empowered by agreement?

- Specifically, what does it mean to "agree" with a spiritual force?

- "Most of us do not need to be convinced that evil is real and operates in our world today, but we need to be clear that evil is a spiritual entity, not just a bad circumstance" (page 205). What are the two extreme views concerning evil?

- Why is it important to neither deny nor become overly focused on evil?

- Read Ephesians 6:10-18 (or refer to the description on page 206). What is our role and God's role in spiritual warfare?

Group Response – *Pray and ask the Holy Spirit to give you spiritual "eyes" to see the true root of the obstacles that you face.*

THINK ABOUT IT

As you read this chapter and engaged in the discussion, what challenged or changed your thinking most? Why?

_____

_____

_____

_____

Our feelings reveal the truth about what we believe. Ask the Holy Spirit to show you the underlying beliefs that your feelings are revealing, and write down what comes to mind.

_____

_____

_____

_____

One of the primary tactics of the enemy is to work covertly. As you read this chapter, what real issues did the Lord show you that you are facing?

_____

_____

_____

_____

_____

Even if you have not fully processed it yet, consider what obstacles "struck a chord" with you as you read. For example, concerning spiritual agreements you may have thought: *"I've made an agreement with the Enemy that says no one cares about me."* Write down what comes to mind.

_____

_____

_____

_____

_____

_____

For each type of obstacle, take a few minutes to ask the Holy Spirit to show you what He wants you to see differently in your life, and write down what comes to mind. (He may not speak to you about every type, but ask Him about each kind and wait for His response.)

- Core lies:

_____

_____

_____

- Soul wounds/trauma:

_____

_____

_____

_____

- Life patterns:

_____

_____

_____

_____

- Spiritual obstacles:

_____

_____

_____

_____

"God Himself must help replace the lie with the truth. The antidote to a lie is not information; it is experiencing the love of the One who is the Truth" (page 200). For each thing that you wrote down above, ask the Holy Spirit to speak His truth to your heart. Write down what He says and ask Him to restore your heart in these areas.

_____

_____

_____

_____

_____

_____

_____

_____

_____

_____

"But seek first his kingdom and his righteousness, and all these things will be given to you as well" (Matthew 6:33, NIV).

Write a brief prayer to the Holy Spirit to continue His work of healing and restoration in your heart. Express your desire to know Him, above all else.

_____

_____

_____

_____

_____

_____

KEY TAKEAWAYS

- What you think are the real issues may not be the real issues. The real obstacles in your life are within you.

- Only God's Spirit at work within you can bring your different parts into unity.

- God's love is the antidote for the lies in your heart.

- The disconnected soul tries to heal itself, but can only rearrange itself around a wound.

- Spiritual forces are empowered by agreement.

- You are in a war every day.

Chapter Eleven
Common Entanglements

As we untangle our mind, our will and our emotions, we rediscover the blueprint for our original design and discover that it is easier to become our true selves than it is to continue being the person we thought we were.

TALK ABOUT IT

- What stood out to you most in this chapter? Why?

- Which of the entanglements named in this chapter were new to you?

- Which were most pertinent to you? Why?

- The enemy has no creative power; he can only take what God has intended for good and twist it. Look back at the entanglements named in this chapter. What is the original, redemptive "untangled" purpose for each one? For example, *forgiveness is a gift that enables the nature of God (love) to be expressed in and through us.*

- When we are saved, our spirit is immediately made new. However, the transformation of our soul is progressive. We must consciously yield to God. When you hear the word *yield* or *submit*, what feelings or images immediately come to mind?

- Why do you think you respond that way?

- Based on what you know about the nature of God, why would He ask you to *yield,* or *submit,* your will to Him?

- Why do all inner vows entangle us in some way, even those we may think are "good inner vows," such as, "I will never ask for money"?

- Upon whose will do we make inner vows, whether we think the vows are "good" or not?

- What did you feel as you read the description of real forgiveness?

- Did you identify with any of the common behaviors that are mistakenly believed to be forgiveness, such as denial or repression? For example, you may have realized that, when trying to "be forgiving" that you have simply minimized or dismissed the wrongs that have been done to you rather than truly address them.

- Describe a time when you truly forgave someone and released them from your judgment. What did you experience before you forgave?

- What did you experience afterward?

- We may connect with another person in an inappropriate way mentally, emotionally, spiritually, or physically. Think about friendships, parent-child relationships, romantic relationships, etc. What are some examples of how someone can be inappropriately connected with another person?

- Did you pray the prayers at the end of each section of this chapter of the book? What did you experience as a result?

- "As we untangle our mind, our will and our emotions, we rediscover the blueprint for our original design and discover that it is easier to become our true selves than it is to continue being the person we thought we were" (page 216). Have you discovered this to be true in your life? In what way?

Group Response – *Ask God to give you insight into the different ways you may be "entangled," and ask Him to set you free.*

_____

_____

_____

_____

_____

THINK ABOUT IT

Ask the Holy Spirit to guide you as you pray through the entanglements. It is not necessary to go through them in the order given; ask the Holy Spirit to show you the right place to start. You may or may not discover something specific to pray about for each entanglement, but be sure to wait on the Lord about each kind and allow Him to speak to your heart.

Generational Transmission:

Ask the Holy Spirit to show you anything that has been passed on to you through your family history. Listen, and write down what comes to mind.

_____

_____

_____

_____

_____

Say out loud, "God, thank you for showing me these things. Please sever the connection between me and the source of these issues."

_____

_____

_____

_____

_____

_____

_____

_____

Ask God to show you what is true about you now that you are a new creation. Write down your thoughts or impressions.

_____

_____

_____

_____

_____

_____

_____

_____

_____

_____

_____

_____

Inner Vows and Judgments

Ask the Holy Spirit to identify any places where you have exercised your will to make an inner vow or judgment. Inner vows are often evidenced by the use of the keyword *will* ("I will …", "I will never … ", "No one will … "). A sign of a judgment may be a hardened heart toward a specific person, type of person, or character trait, such as men, women, authority figures, poor people, etc. Write down anything that comes to mind.

_____

_____

_____

_____

_____

_____

_____

Tell God that you recognize that you set your will and took control through each inner vow (specifically tell Him what things you have taken control of and the vows you recognize), and ask Him to forgive you for using your will in a wrong way and damaging your own soul. Renounce your inner vow or judgment.

_____

_____

_____

_____

_____

_____

_____

_____

_____

Ask God to speak to you about His ability to protect you and write down the impressions that come to mind.

_____

_____

_____

_____

_____

Unforgiveness

Ask the Holy Spirit to help you make the difficult decision to forgive those who have hurt, damaged, mistreated, or abused you. You may want to read pages 224-227 of the book to refresh your memory about what forgiveness is, what it is not, and its purpose. For each hurt or offense, pray something like the following:

Lord, today I choose to forgive _____ and give them back to you. I will live the rest of my life with what they have done to me and not hold it against them anymore. I forgive them for _____. When they did these things to me, I felt _____. I release these feelings to You now, Lord, and ask that you would bring Your healing touch to my heart."

As you pray through each hurtful situation, ask the Holy Spirit to help you release your hurt and the painful feelings it has caused. You may experience strong emotions, but do not rush the process or release your feelings only in your mind. God will heal your heart as you fully release the hurt and anger to Him.

Ask the Lord to speak to you and show you His heart for you right now, at this moment. Write down what you believe He is saying.

_____

_____

_____

_____

_____

Unhealthy Connections

Ask the Holy Spirit to make you aware of any connections with others that you need break, whether they were formed by your choice or the choice of another person. Wait quietly for Him to speak to you, and write down the connections that come to mind.

_____

_____

_____

_____

_____

_____

Confess your unhealthy connections to God by naming the person with whom you have an unhealthy connection and the specific choices or actions that you committed that led to the unhealthy connection. Ask Him to forgive you and cleanse you from your role in establishing the unhealthy connection, and ask Him to sever it.

Ask the Lord to show you who He meant for you to be, separate from that person or connection. Write down what He shows you.

_____

_____

_____

_____

_____

Contact

Acknowledge that you can only access the Holy Spirit through Jesus, and ask the Holy Spirit to show you any times that you accessed the spiritual realm through any other means. Write down what comes to mind.

_____

_____

_____

_____

_____

_____

_____

_____

_____

_____

Confess to God that you have allowed yourself to have contact with the spiritual arena in an unholy way, and name the specific choices or actions through which you have done so. Tell Him you are sorry, and ask Him to forgive you. Ask Him to cleanse and free you of anything that has impacted you, and to remove any spiritual force that entered your soul as a result of your actions.

_____

_____

_____

_____

_____

_____

Invite the Holy Spirit to fill you with His presence, and to shine His light on every dark place. Ask Him what He would like to do in your life, and write down what He says.

_____

_____

_____

_____

_____

_____

_____

_____

_____

_____

_____

_____

- Entanglements tie up your soul in a way that makes it difficult to move forward. They are things that were originally good that are twisted and used against you.

- Family traits, both positive and negative, can be passed down from one generation to the next.

- Inner vows and judgments activate your will in a self-protective way, causing a "lockdown" in the soul.

- Chronic anger and bitterness are common and effective strategies that the enemy uses to keep you from becoming who you were meant to be.

- The instruction to forgive others is not an unreasonable demand but a key to freedom.

- You may develop unhealthy connections with others mentally, spiritually, physically, or emotionally that hinder your growth.

- You can only access the spiritual realm through Jesus. By accessing it through any other means, you open yourself up to spirits that are not the Holy Spirit and only have your destruction in mind.

Chapter Twelve
Making All Things New / Epilogue

It is entirely about Him, but in the midst of His own story He comes to us and tells us our story matters to Him, along with all of its details … Our stories are intertwined. We become people whose lives display His story.

TALK ABOUT IT

- Over the course of reading this book, what has the Lord shown you that has changed your way of thinking the most? Why?

- When you consider the span and scope of God's story, how does it make you feel to realize that He walks with you personally—that *your* story matters?

- How would you have defined freedom before reading this book?

- How do you define freedom now?

- In what ways are you now living in greater freedom than before?

- "We must not confuse the diligent pursuit of fulfilling our destiny with some kind of performance upon which God's love or approval hinges" (page 243). Based on what you understand about the nature of God's character, how does God view the pursuit of fulfilling our destiny?

- How does He want us to approach the pursuit?

- "He was *very* good. But something more than talent and skill came through his performance … This man was fully alive and living in sheer exultation as he effortlessly conquered this trapeze. He was doing the very thing he was born to do" (page 249).

- Who has most inspired you to discover yourself?

- What is it that you find inspiring about them? Why?

- What have you discovered about yourself lately that has been most surprising to you?

Group Response – *Together, thank God for all He has done in and through you over the course of this study. Ask Him to continue working in your lives over the coming weeks and months.*

_____

_____

_____

_____

THINK ABOUT IT

Write a brief letter to God, expressing how you have felt about your journey so far, and your desire to be part of His greater story.

_____

_____

_____

_____

_____

_____

Ask God what He is saying in response to your letter, and write down your impressions.

_____
_____
_____
_____
_____
_____

Who does God say that you are?

_____
_____
_____
_____
_____
_____

What is the thing that you were created to do?

_____
_____
_____
_____
_____
_____
_____

KEY TAKEAWAYS

- The story is not about you, but you are part of the story. Your story displays His.

- The focus of your journey is not removing obstacles, but reconnecting with your Source and the greater story.

- Your quest to fulfill your destiny is not a performance upon which God's love and approval hinges.

- When others see you walking in freedom, it sparks a desire for freedom and ignites change in their own lives.

Appendix

The following is a step-by-step guide to help you discover what core belief about your identity may be driving your behavior (action). It will also help you visualize how the impact of your actions and experiences may be feeding that belief.

To discover the core belief about your identity, you will start with the action you would like to change, and work both backward and forward from there, uncovering the cause and effect of the behavior. Remember to invite the Holy Spirit to guide your thinking throughout the exercise.

As you follow the instructions, write your answers in the appropriate boxes in the table below. (You may want to make a few copies so you can use the table multiple times.)

Identity	
Perception	
Desire	

Choice	
Action	
Experience	
Impact	

1. Action

In this box, write the behavior, emotional state, or emotional reaction that you wish were different. For example, *I lose control of my temper and yell at my family.*

2. Choice

What is your *will* focused on just prior to acting in the way you described? This is not listing the choice to act in the way you described, but the position of your *will*. Examples: *I chose to take things personally; I chose to dwell on negative thoughts; I chose to be in a place that supported destructive or harmful actions; I chose to assume the worst.*

In the box, write the choice of the will that you made prior to behaving in the way you would like to change.

3. Desire

What do you desire? This is not the desire to change the action in question, but the desire you are trying to satisfy *through* the action. The undesirable action is what you have believed to be a solution to a state of discomfort, pain, or frustration (albeit, not an effective solution). For example, the alcoholic doesn't desire alcohol *first;* they desire relief from pain. A person struggling with control doesn't simply desire control, but to alleviate their fear. A parent does not scream at their children because they desire to scream; they scream because they desire response and change.

In the appropriate box, write what you really desire.

4. Perception

What do you sense is happening? How does the circumstance make you feel? What relational dynamic or problem are you sensing that is leading you to desire a solution? Examples: *I am being unfairly criticized; My opinion is being ignored; I am being judged without an opportunity to defend myself.*

In the box, write what you sense is happening (or not happening) concerning you, leading up to your action.

5. Experience

In this box, write what you experience immediately following the action you described. How do you feel after you act? How does your action affect your self-perception? For example, *After I lose my temper and yell at my family, I feel guilty and that I'm a bad parent.*

Note that self-destructive actions feed our perceptions; for example, shame is an experience wrought by poor choices and harmful actions, and feeds directly into the way every person perceives themselves.

6. Impact

In this box, write the effect of your action on you and the people in your relational circle. How does your experience (*i.e.*, shame, self-loathing, frustration, guilt) affect your self-perception?

When your negative behavior becomes the source of your self-perception, it significantly increases the power of this cycle to lead you again to the very behavior or emotional state that you wish you would change. This is how self-destructive behavior becomes self-maintaining—when the impact of your action or emotional state begins to tell you *who you are*.

Consider this: What if these choices are actually the result of your misperceptions and *not* the result of something that is fundamentally true about you?

7. Identity

Study your answers in the other boxes (especially "perception"). What belief about your identity do they point toward, true or not?

For example, imagine that you answered in the following way:

Action—*I yell at my spouse*
Choice—*I assume the worst about their motives*
Desire—*To make myself heard*
Perception—*No one listens to my opinion.*

These answers could point to this belief about your identity: *My views and feelings are not valuable.*

In the box, write the misconception about your identity that is likely the driving force behind the cycle (perception, desire, choice, action, experience, and impact).

It is important to realize that what *is* true about you and what you *perceive* to be true about you may not be the same. The Parable of the Acrobat is designed to illustrate how your perceptions can actually rob you of the truth about your true identity, and by so doing, completely hijack your experience.

8. **Truth**

Repeat the exercise, beginning with your identity, but this time, write what *is* true about you from God's point of view. If you were to accept and agree with this truth, what would you then perceive? What would you desire? What choice would you make? What action would you choose? What would you likely experience afterward? What impact would it have on you, others, and your circumstances?

Ask God to make His truth your new reality.